WELFARE MOTHERS GOURMET COOKBOOK

How to make sumpin out of nothin

Carol Flemming

authorHOUSE

AuthorHouse™
1663 Liberty Drive
Bloomington, IN 47403
www.authorhouse.com
Phone: 833-262-8899

Published by AuthorHouse 12/07/2020

ISBN: 978-1-6655-0856-8 (sc)
ISBN: 978-1-6655-0857-5 (hc)
ISBN: 978-1-6655-0855-1 (e)

Chinarose's input:

"I am grateful to be able to pass on to my children your skills and passion for food and nutrition, as well as your love of quality family time in the kitchen. Those who take the time to bond over food, grow food, and enjoy food together are a blessed and wise group."

Chinarose, daughter

Monah's input:

"I've been an adult now for many years, and I've still never tasted possum stew or pigeon pie or whatever Mom was catching in the backyard. You can't make me eat it, Mom!"

"I've never been an adventurous person when it comes to trying new foods and

delicacies. But Mom always said, 'Just try it, you might like it.' Sometimes I was pleasantly surprised, and sometimes, I got busted trying to get the

dog to eat it! Oh well, at least I tried it."

Monah, daughter

Martie's introduction:

Carol has been my best friend for most of my life. Nearly two years into our friendship, Carol mentioned to me that she knew where Neil Young lived and that it was his birthday. What a great opportunity to make him a surprise birthday cake, as I had a little crush on him. So off to the kitchen we went. We decided to make a pound cake. It was then sliced into layers, filled with a creamy chocolate icing, covered with whipped cream, and dotted with raspberries and shaved chocolate. Whew! It was a perfect birthday cake for Neil Young. We were both very pleased.

My daughter and I were staying with Carol and her children at the time in her old Victorian house that she saved from being condemned. Our main modes of transportation were biking or hitchhiking. Hitchhiking with a cake, from Santa Cruz up the coast to La Honda, sounded totally doable, sure; it would be another fun adventure with Carol. We had heard that it might rain, but we were optimistic that it would miss us. Unfortunately, it didn't. It started to rain and continued to get worse. We weren't even out of the driveway yet. We tried to think of ways to protect the cake from the heavy rain. Carol looked like a drowned rat standing there, and I knew I looked the same. I was so disappointed and sad that I wasn't going to meet Neil Young and give him his surprise birthday cake. Suddenly Carol looked at me with a twinkle in her eyes and said in her own Carol-like way, "fuck it, let's go back inside and have some fun." She then called some friends to come over and celebrate Neil Young's birthday with us and share the cake. It turned out to be a fun afternoon anyway, and all agreed that the cake was absolutely delicious.

This is one of many memorable moments I've shared with Carol. She has taught me so much during our long friendship, and I am so grateful to her. The book is full of anecdotes, helpful hints, and a lot of laughs. I hope you all enjoy Carol's stories and adventures in cooking and gardening on a budget in this book. – Martie Ochs

For my children: Beau, Patty, Monah, Lisa, Nancy, & Chinarose

"Mom, I'm hungry!" Feeding your family is the most important thing you can do as a mother. After that, it's teaching right from wrong and getting them to stand on their own two feet--then you kick them out of the house, and redecorate and rent their room.

BREAKFAST

It's the most important meal, so they say.

Oatmeal

Oatmeal is one of those stick-to-your-ribs foods that hold you up for hours. Besides, it's cheaper than artificially sweetened cereal that is expensive and addicting--not good. You can vary the oatmeal and make it more interesting and nourishing by adding chopped fruit such as apples, bananas, and raisins. Or you can make extra and save the leftover oatmeal. Put it in a bowl overnight and then, the next morning, turn it out, slice it like bread, fry it, and serve it with syrup. It's crispy on the outside and soft on the inside.

Pancakes

Pancakes are just flour, milk, and eggs. If you make the batter really thin, it's a crepe, and you can roll the fruit inside it and top with a spoon of homemade jam. What kid wouldn't eat that?

Jam

Homemade jam--apples, apricots, berries, peaches, strawberries, grapes. Plums are my favorite. Take whatever is in season, and put it in a pot with a cup of sugar and enough water to barely cover it. Simmer for a long time, a couple of hours, until it reduces.

Some fruits need pectin; get a package from the grocery store or a Wal-Mart in the canning section. But plums don't need pectin, nor do most berries. (The tarter the fruit is, the more pectin it's liable to have.) In another large pot, put your jars that you have been saving (or that you found at a thrift store) and the lids, bring to a boil, and reduce heat. Do this before your jam is ready! With tongs, remove the jar. Careful, don't burn yourself; steam burns are nasty! Using a spoon, ladle the jam from the pot into the jars, use tongs to put the lids on, and twist them partially closed with a towel. When they cool, you can tighten them fully. This sterilizes the jars and keeps your precious jam from growing blue-and-green science-project stuff.

The difference between jam and jelly is that jam has the whole fruit, and jam is clear. Its best to put up enough jam and jelly during the summer to carry you through the winter.

French toast

Beat a couple of eggs with some milk and a teaspoon of vanilla, and dip your sliced bread (not too thick and not too thin) into it. Don't let it get soggy. Ugh! Fry in a frying pan, preferably cast iron, until golden brown on both sides. Now take it out and cut it to form triangles on the plate (it's prettier than a plain square). Add some fruit on the side, and voila, a beautiful breakfast. You can go overboard and sprinkle some powdered sugar on it, but I don't want my kids to have sugar. There's plenty of sugar in the fruit. Butter is nice if you have it. A little butter goes a long way. Never use margarine, it's like feeding your kids plastic bags--don't do it.

Soft- and hard-boiled eggs

The incredible eatable egg can be used in so many ways. My mother used to fry them in bacon grease until they were hard and greasy. I remember sitting in front of an egg that I refused to eat for an hour while my mother glared at me and kept saying (through gritted teeth) "Eat it!" I gagged. Finally, she let me go. I have never made my children eat anything they didn't want to.

Ah, but an egg is ok if it's a soft-boiled egg in a glass. I don't know where it came from, but it was a family thing. Try it. Take a handful of soda crackers, crush them in a glass, and add a pat of butter, Put an egg in boiling water for three minutes, and then scoop onto the crackers and salt and pepper and mix it up with a spoon. It looks terrible but tastes great.

Eggs are very delicate. Most people tend to overcook them. To cook hard-boiled eggs, start them in cold water, bring it to a boil, and turn it off. Let them sit for 20 minutes, and they are done—no need to cook them for twenty minutes, and you save energy. Peel them under cold water.

One egg on a slice of toast will carry almost anyone through the morning. I like to fry my egg in butter and not butter the toast. See, I told you a little butter goes a long way. If you can't afford butter, hard-boil them. When we lived where it snowed, on cold mornings, I would hard-boil eggs and give them to the kids to put in their pockets as hand warmers to be eaten later for a snack with a tiny tin of salt.

Hurry-up company dinner, or brunch frittata

Sauté any vegetables you have in the fridge in a cast iron or ovenproof pan, Use onions, of course, and zucchini and tomatoes are pretty. Add celery/parsley/squash, and put in some herbs. Thyme is always good with eggs, or try dill. Add salt and pepper. Grate and add any cheese you may have, or add scrambled eggs with the cheese and milk in equal parts. Put it in the oven at 350 till the eggs are firm and golden. Take it out of the oven, put the pan on the table (with a trivet underneath it!), and serve it with French bread and a bottle of white wine. Delicious and quick.

EATING FROM THE GARDEN

If you have a little more space, plant a garden; a $2.00 packet of seeds can grow a bushel of carrots. What's up, Doc! Beets are lovely, and kale is very easy to grow and very good for you. If you don't have space, grow things in containers on windowsills. Small herb pots of chives, oregano, thyme, parsley, and basil will make you a gourmet cook. Rosemary is a shrub that can be found in lots of gardens. You may not need to plant your own if the neighbors already have it growing. It is a dusty blue-green with little blue flowers.

Growing herbs is fun and easy. Use any container with a hole in the bottom for drainage. Tin cans can make lovely containers. Take a large nail and a hammer, turn it upside down, and pound your aggressions away. Make three or four holes and fill the pot with soil. Come on, you can find some dirt somewhere. If you can afford it, buy potting soil. If not, dig up some soil from a vacant lot or parks.

Parks are not off-limits, and they're good for flower cuttings too. It's best to cut in the early morning. When I was first married, I lived across from a city park. My house was always filled with fresh flowers. In the early morning, walk in the park with scissors in your pocket. If you really want to get into it, you can start with cuttings. Geraniums are everywhere and come in many colors. When you go geranium hunting, take a container and some wet paper. Break off a five- or six-inch new stem from the plant, wrap it in the paper, and bring it home. Put the stem in water and keep it in the kitchen window. Keep the water fresh by changing it every few days, and soon roots will appear from the torn part. You can plant it in one to two weeks. (You can put the cut stems directly in the soil, but it's better to give them a start in water.)

You can eat the petals of many flowers such as pansies, marigolds, nasturtiums, chrysanthemums, hibiscus, and daylilies. They are pretty in salads. If you are not acquainted with these flowers, go online and look up edible flowers. If you don't have a computer or electricity, for that matter, go to the library. Library cards are free, and since you are a welfare mom and not tied to a job, take the kids with you. While you do the research, it could be useful for them. Now you have your pot garden--no pun intended. (OK, yes, it's a pun.) We are not talking cash crop here but rather feeding your family--we'll get into the other kind of gardening later.

Speaking of weed, purslane is a common weed that you have probably been walking on for years. It grows close to the ground between sidewalks, and has little yellow flowers. It spreads like wildfire. Cultivate it; it tastes something like celery. It will grow anywhere--in pots is fine. While it's green, before it flowers, snip off a few stems. Chop it and throw it in a salad, or sauté with a little olive oil, butter, and a dash of soy sauce, and serve as a side vegetable. It's high in omega-three and has potassium and magnesium. I eat it raw, like a bunny. Your chickens will love it too.

BREAD

Staff of life bread

Learn to make bread. It's easy—basically, flour and water. And a little bit of yeast. OK, here's a basic bread recipe. First thing in the morning, put two cups of lukewarm water in a nonabrasive bowl, ceramic or glass. Add a "scant" of yeast. (A scant is what you can hold in the palm of your hand, or enough to lightly cover the water in the bowl. About a tablespoon, if you are more comfortable with measurements--I usually eyeball everything.) Add a couple of pinches of salt and some sugar. Sugar helps to activate the yeast.

Now walk away and do something else. Pour yourself a cup of tea, wash last night's dishes. Come back in five minutes and stir slightly with (and this is important) a wooden spoon. If you don't have one, get one at a second-hand store. Wooden spoons are essential for bread making. Now add about two to three cups of flour. Unbleached is better than white. But it costs more--don't ask me why. Stir the flour into the water a little bit at a time. This is where your arms get a workout. Keep adding flour until the dough is stiff enough to handle without it oozing when you put it on a floured board. And then you knead it. Flour your hands and fold it into itself repeatedly, pushing it down, until it forms into a smooth ball. Then put it in a warm oiled bowl. Cover it with a dishtowel, clean up the flour mess, drink your coffee, and feed the dog, cats, and kids. Maybe take a shower.

When the bread rises to double in size, take it out of the bowl and put it back on the floured board. Oh no, did you wash the board? Don't until you are all done. And knead it some more. This is how you get air in the dough, by making a strong framework that can hold the bubbles. Put it back in the oiled bowl and let it rise a second time. Do something else--yoga, smoke a ciggy. When it's up over the top of the bowl, knead it again on the floured board and divide it into two round balls. You can form long loaves or round loaves.

Put the loaves in a greased baking pan and let them rise again; then pop them into the oven at 350 and wait till they are golden brown and smell like bread. And voila! you got bread. Now there are several variations on this bread. For example, you can add more sugar to the dough. Melt some butter into a round baking pan. Cut the dough into ten to twelve pieces and round each one by holding it in one hand and pushing it through your thumb and forefinger with the other hand. Fill the pan with these little dough rounds and sprinkle with chopped walnuts (or any kind of nuts you have) and a handful of brown sugar. Let it rise again and pop it in the oven until it's light brown and smells yummy. Now you have pull-apart sweet rolls that your kids will love.

Or you can add some chicken stock into the warm water when you start the dough. Go out into the garden and gather a handful of herbs that you have growing there or from the pots in the windowsill. Chives, parsley, rosemary, dill--whatever you've got. With these, you can turn your dough into savory herb bread. Dried herbs are OK, but those fresh ones that you planted and that are doing so well will make excellent bread. To make mixed-grain bread, add oatmeal, bran, wheat germ, whole-grain flour, and a little molasses. Good bread in stores will cost you three to five dollars and will most likely contain preservatives. Never eat anything with ingredients you cannot pronounce--they are not good for you. And stay away from corn glucose, which is in almost everything. Read the labels, buy large quantities of flour and yeast with your food stamps, and you will always have bread on the table.

Quick breads

Irish soda bread

If you have a Dutch oven, bake this in it. If not, a pie pan will do. The oven temperature is 450, hotter than usual.

4 cups all-purpose flour

1 tsp. salt

1 tsp. baking soda

1 tsp. sugar

¼ c shortening (Crisco, oil, butter, or lard—lard makes the best piecrust ever)

1 2/3 c buttermilk

I always like to sift my flour because sometimes there can be lumps in it. Rub this mixture together with your fingers. You washed them before starting, didn't you? Add the shortening. Make a hollow in the center of the flour mixture and pour the buttermilk into it. (If you do not have buttermilk, do this before you start: take a cup of milk and add a tablespoon of white vinegar or lemon juice, let it set, and you have buttermilk. White vinegar is cheap and can be used for many things--cleaning your windows is one. White vinegar and water is less expensive than Windex and does a better job.)

Anyway, stir slightly with a fork until the dough comes together. Turn it out on a floured surface and knead several times until dough is smooth. Shape it into a ball and place it smooth-side up in a well-greased pan. Cut a cross in the top of the loaf. Cover the Dutch oven or pan and put it in the oven for 10 minutes at 450; then reduce the heat to 350 and bake for 45 minutes or until golden brown. Serve warm. Easy smeecy!

Fruit breads

When the bananas are turning or when they're on the dollar rack at the store, it's an excellent time to make banana bread.

1 ½ cups flour

1 tsp. baking soda

1tsp. salt

(I haven't measured anything in years; I just eyeball it. But if you are a beginner baker, this is foolproof.)

Sift the dry stuff into a bowl. Then, in another bowl, mix 1/3 cup oil and ¾ cup brown sugar. (If you don't have brown sugar, add a tablespoon of molasses to white sugar.) Add 1 cup mashed bananas (from three or four bananas), two eggs, and

1/3 cup milk. Stir everything together and pour into a greased bread pan. You can add nuts of any kind. (No, not peanuts. That's weird. Well, OK, if you chop them finely. Still, walnuts are better.)

Bake for about 1 hour or until a toothpick comes out clean from the middle. Turn the bread out of the pan and let it sit until it cools. It will finish cooking during that time. If you get hungry and cut into it now, it will probably fall apart, so do something else and come back in an hour. You can add apples instead of bananas, and some cinnamon and ginger. If no fruit is available, just put in some of your sweet spices and make a spice bread. Molasses is good, and so are cinnamon, cloves, and nutmeg. (Be careful with cloves. They are powerful, so just a little will do.)

Now you have a sweet bread that's good with tea. Did we talk about tea? Mint is so easy to grow. You can pull it out of the ground, forget it for a day, and stick it in the dirt. Water it, and it will start a whole family. Keep it in a container, or it will take over the entire garden. Mint makes a great tea, especially iced tea in the summer. Keep a pitcher in the fridge instead of lemonade.

Sourdough

Sourdough takes a little longer but is worth it. I used to make two loaves every day, one for my family and one for a friend who had lived in France. He said it was as good as any French bread he ever had. He would come by around noon, bring a bottle of gin, and we would have a drink or two with conversation while he waited for his bread. To make the starter, you must have a crock or glass bowl. Search in second-hand stores until you find a small crock like Grandma's. Stainless steel will not work. Combine 2 cups warm water with one scant of active dry yeast, one tablespoon sugar, and two cups flour. Beat well, cover loosely with a clean cloth, and put in a quiet, warm place. If you have a gas stove with a pilot light, that's great. In the summer, almost anyplace out of the way will do, such as the top of the fridge. (Feel it to see if it's warm. Not hot, just a steady room temperature.) The temperature is the most crucial thing about a bread starter.

Once it gets started, you can keep it in the fridge, but for the first week, stir it a couple of times a day with a wooden spoon, never metal. In about three days, it will start to smell sour. Good! When you are ready to add the flour in your bread recipe, add only half of the starter. Replenish the leftover starter with more of the same flour and water, cover it, and let it sit for another day. The older your starter is, the better your bread will be. Remember to stir it and always keep it covered with a cloth. If it bubbles a bit, it's even better. If you want a crusty loaf, brush the loaf with water before you put it in the oven.

Garlic bread

If you have butter, smash the garlic into the butter (you can add some olive oil too). Slice a loaf of bread lengthways and cut it almost all the way through into pieces. Spread the mix on it. If you have a little Parmesan, sprinkle it on top. Put it under the broiler until it is slightly golden. Do not walk away. Watch it, and take it out when it is golden, not brown and burnt. Soup and bread, what more could you want? A bottle of wine, maybe.

YOGURT

Mix 3 tablespoons of unflavored store-bought yogurt with four cups milk (you can use dried milk). Scald the milk, or bring it to a boil and let it cool. Put it in an ice bath in the sink, or in a bowl of ice. Let it cool; do not disturb it for 4-10 hours. (It's best made at night before you go to bed.) The next morning, pour it into a mason jar or ceramic container. (This is important--no metal bowls.) Cover and refrigerate 2 to 3 hours. At this point, you can add flavoring--vanilla, fruit jam, or real fresh fruit. Nuts are good.

BEANS

Spend your money wisely; buy quantities of flour, beans, and rice. Beans, the magical fruit: the more you eat, the more you toot. High in protein, better for you than most meat unless it's organic or grass-fed. Don't get me started on how bad meat is for you. It's full of things you do not want to eat and it will make you fat, possibly give you cancer. As I said, don't get me started. If you like, read *Forks over knives*. It's an easy read, and you will get some clues about what you are putting in your body. I always said you are what you eat. Do you really want to be a fat cow? So back to beans.

My grandmother said you should soak them overnight in cold water (that's after you take the rocks out.) Nowadays, the beans come clean and don't have to be soaked overnight, except it saves cooking time by a little.

Pinto beans are the most popular for chili and Mexican beans in a big pot. Cover with double the water because they are going to puff up. You can soak if you like, or just start them in the morning. Add one large onion or two small ones. (Yellow onions are cheaper. I don't know why.) Use whatever is available and a handful of garlic cloves (peeled, of course). Bring to a boil and turn to low. Let cook for two hours. For a large pot, use one package of dried beans or about two cups if you are buying them in bags of 25 or 50 lbs., which you should be.

Mexican markets and Asian markets have better prices, especially on rice. It's worth going across town once a month. I start almost everything I make with onions and garlic, except for apple pie. Now that you have your basic beans, depending on your mood, make something.

Chili

Chili is great in the winter. Along with your garlic and onions, add some cayenne pepper, paprika, cumin, black pepper, dried red chilies, and hamburger if you want it (or you can fool the kids by adding a cup of oatmeal; it cooks to the same texture as hamburger). You can add tomato sauce and oregano, plus just a little chili powder. Cook for hours (usually two) on simmer. Serve with chopped onion and a little cheese on top, or add your herbs and spices.

You can also make bean soup with oregano, rosemary, thyme, whatever you have. To make it Mexican, add oregano, chili powder, cayenne, and red peppers. Never add salt till the last, and then add it to taste. A pot of beans on the stove smells good and can be served alone in a bowl.

If you have the makings for salsa, add some. (See the salsa recipe later in this book.)

FREE FOOD

Take a walk in your neighborhood or ride your bicycle. You will be surprised at how many fruit trees there are. And the strange thing is that the people who own them seldom pick them. If you look carefully, you will find plums, apricots, peaches, nuts, apples, and berries.

I found a star fruit tree. Pretty amazing! The owners did not even know what it was or what to do with the fruit. It was delicious. Ted, a surfer friend of mine, lived almost entirely off of free fruit. He cruised around Santa Cruz on his old bike with a wooden box wired to the handlebars and collected fruit. If the tree was on the street, it was fair game. If it was in a yard, he would simply ask whoever answered the door if he could have some. I've done that with Meyer lemons--the owner even asked me if I wanted a bag. "Take all you want," she said, and I did, and I returned again and again. Lemons make lemonade, lemon meringue pie, lemon bars, and salad dressing. Great stuff! Plums make excellent jam and are just fine in a bowl for after-school snacks.

If you live in a rural area, have a car, and take a drive, you will find walnut trees along the highways in the fall. When they drop on the ground, they are fair game. Take a sack or old pillowcase, and wear gloves because walnuts stain your hands and the stain will linger for days. Walnuts come with a green husk. Gather lots of them, and they will last all winter. Take them home and spread them out to dry outside or in a safe, warm place. The green husk will crack open, and then you can peel them. Walnuts are great for baking.

Pesto

Pesto is usually made from pine nuts, but pine nuts are very expensive, and walnuts work just fine. Put the nuts in a blender or food processor with some olive oil and some of those basil leaves you have growing at the back door, and blend. Add a little salt. Refrigerated, it will last for weeks. It's great on any kind of pasta or spread on some of that homemade bread.

1 clove garlic

¼ cup nuts

3 cups basil

½ cup olive oil

1 oz. parmesan

Salt and pepper

Apples

Now, if you can find an apple orchard, jackpot! I met a woman with an apple orchard, and she invited my family to pick as much as we wanted. If you wrap apples in newspaper and put them in a box in a cool dark place like a garage or basement, they will last for months. But remember, one bad apple spoils the bunch. That's why you wrap them in paper, because if one goes bad, it does not taint the others. You can make apple pie, apple crisp, even apple juice if you are lucky enough to own a juicer. I got mine in a thrift store--new, still in the box. A two-hundred-dollar juicer for thirty-five dollars! You can do some healthy stuff with a juicer.

You can make apple cake, applesauce (mmm), and of course, keep fresh apples on the table for after-school snacks. Though we had little money when my kids were growing up, there was always fruit on the table, soup on the stove, and bread in the oven.

SOUPS

Pebble soup

Fill a large pot with water. (Not aluminum--if you have aluminum, throw it out! Bad stuff, hurts your brain. Cast iron is the best and lasts forever. Stainless steel is OK. Copper is overrated, and who wants to spend hours polishing copper? Though it looks nice and a chef friend of mine swears by it, it's expensive, and we are talking about people on a budget.) Into the pot of water, throw a handful of medium-sized pebbles, washed, from the garden. Then go to the fridge and pull out everything you can find that could go into soup: onions, garlic, celery, any other vegetables. Chop tomatoes and throw them in. Sausage, ham, bacon (fry it first). Go to the cupboard and find some herbs: oregano, thyme, and rosemary are always good. You can add a can of tomato paste or some catsup for color and sweetness. Beans are great too, and so is rice. Now bring it to a boil and drop the heat to simmer. The longer you simmer, the better the flavor. Now (important!) with a large slotted spoon, take the pebbles out and throw them back in the garden. Voila! Pebble soap. Serve with your homemade bread—it's a nourishing meal.

Ramen

This is a staple in many low-budget homes. It can be made into something fantastic by following the directions. Put it in water, silly. Then chop all the vegetables in the fridge and add them on top before serving. It's Asian soup and salad together.

Borscht

Now for my all-time favorite. My kids hated it till they grew up-- and then they asked for the recipe.

Take a large head of red cabbage, six or eight large beets, and two red onions. Slice or chop it all and simmer in the pot with a minimal amount of oil. Then add enough water to fill half the pot. Allow it to simmer two or more hours. Add a little wine vinegar and about a tablespoon of honey for flavor. This soup is a beautiful shade of red. You can keep a pot simmering for days, and it only gets better. Just keep adding water when you serve it, and if you have it, a dollop of sour cream or yogurt. Remember, I taught you to make yogurt already. I love this soup.

Potato soup

Peel and cut any kind of potatoes you have into small cubes. Sauté some onions and garlic in a cast-iron Dutch oven. (It's my preference for almost all cooking, but use a large pot, anyway.) Add yellow or white onions and some celery or purslane and carrots. Don't let them get dark; this is a white soup. Watch it until the onions are transparent. (Oh, forgot to tell you--put the garlic in last because it will cook faster than onions.) Cook slowly and add some chicken stock and a sprig of parsley at the end for color. The next day, if you have soup left over, add two cans of creamed corn, some thyme, butter or cream, and a teaspoon of brown sugar, and you have corn chowder. Or add a bay leaf, two cans of chopped clams, some clam juice, and you have clam chowder.

Minestrone

This is my favorite hearty winter soup. When you have some leftover beef, or pot roast, cut it into mouth-size pieces (depending on how big your mouth is). Sauté your standard vegetables (onions, carrots, celery, garlic) and add your meat.

Now add your herbs (they are better when you brown them with the meat and vegetables): oregano, rosemary, basil, sage, and parsley. You could also add some chopped potatoes, zucchini, and a can of kidney beans. If there is any open red wine, that's always good to add, and a can of tomato paste or sauce. My secret ingredient is catsup. Put in pasta in an amount equal to your potatoes and let it simmer for a long time. Serve with your homemade sourdough bread.

CHICKENS

If you have space to raise a couple of chickens, a lot of cities now allow it. Check out raising chickens online if you know nothing about it. You can buy chickens for two or three dollars, and they will produce one, sometimes two eggs a day. While you are eating oatmeal, the store of eggs will back up, and you will have twice as many. Feed the chickens table scraps, saving money on chicken food. Your chickens will eat what you don't eat: potato peels, eggshells, leftovers that have been in the fridge for three days.

Chickens will eat anything, and especially if it is moldy. My friend Madeline kept one chicken, and it free-ranged during the day. In other words, it was outside in her yard, then came in at night, climbed a ladder to the top of the fridge, and nested there. In the morning, it laid an egg and went back outside, the cutest thing you ever did see. It's also possible to build a small movable cage with no bottom and move it from place to place, keeping your chicken contained and debugging your yard while it fertilizes the soil. Pretty good, huh? If you are going to get serious about chickens, check out a book called *Back to basics*; it will give you a diagram for building a chicken coop.

How to get three meals out of one chicken
First, where did that chicken come from? If you think that chicken comes cut up in packages, let me tell you how it really is.

On the farm, I learned to kill and clean a chicken.

First, you take one of your pet chickens, hold it by its feet, and lay its head on a stump. Then you take an ax and swing hard and hopefully cut its head off on the first try. Otherwise, it's messy. Then you throw the headless chicken under a tin bucket until it's quiet because if it is let go, it will run around "like a chicken with its head cut off"--that's where the expression came from. Then, dunk the dead chicken in boiling hot water and pull its feathers off, holding it upside down. Use tweezers to pull out the pinfeathers to have a smooth, clean chicken.

Here comes the fun part. Take the chicken into the sink and rinse it in cold water. Now stick your hand in its ass and pull out all the guts, which are interesting shades of different colors. Save the gizzard and liver--they are a delicacy to some people. Oh, and don't forget the craw, the sack where the chicken saves what it has eaten, kinda like a stomach. Chickens don't have stomachs. Now, when this is done, give the chicken a bath. Put in a salt-water bath until it's ready to cool. Enough to turn you into a vegetarian, right!? I still can remember my mother being horribly disgusted by the whole process, muttering "Icky! Ahh darn!"

My father was a cook on a merchant marine ship and could crack five eggs in one hand without getting a shell in the omelet. He cooked on the weekends. His mother, my favorite grandmother, whom we called Mom, owned a restaurant in Oakland, called the Country Kitchen. She was a great cook. She taught me to make bread, and the day before I was married, she gave me an iron skillet and a steel chef's knife and told me that was all I needed. But I digress. Here are the three meals.

Meal one: Roast one plump chicken in the oven and boil some potatoes. (They cook faster if you cut them smaller, and that saves on the power bill.) Mash the potatoes after the chicken comes out of the oven, so they are still warm while the chicken rests before you slice into it. I like to rub salt on the chicken before baking it, and if you remember, it's best to soak your chicken in cold salt water overnight before you cook it, then it's Kosher. When roasted, it tastes better, and the salt on the crisp skin is a tasty treat for the cook.

Toss a green salad with whatever is in season and available, like carrots. I like to grate carrots. It looks nice and you don't need as much. Even if it's just lettuce and carrots, that's fine. Red onions sliced thin only takes half an onion. Wrap the other half for later. Tomatoes are great, especially if you are growing your own. Cherry tomatoes, the ones called orange sunshine, are very sweet, flavorful, and easy to grow in a pot at the back door. (For other salads, see the Salads section.)

Kale is also easy to grow. You can keep cutting it, and it will grow back. Kale can be kinda tough, I mean the texture. So it's best picked young. It is one of the highest vegetables on the food chain and great for you. I also put it in soups and chili.

OK. Now take that chicken out of the pan. Put the pan on the top of the stove, and sprinkle some flour in the drippings. Turn up the heat and add a cup of water. Use milk or cream if you want it rich and creamy, or chicken stock, and stir in to make gravy. I use a thing I call a squeegee, a circular springy device to make gravy--can't make it without it. Maybe you can do it with a spoon. Add some milk when it starts to get thick, and salt and pepper. Now you have chicken and gravy.

Make the kids eat their salad first; otherwise they might not eat it at all. And the salad dressing--no bottled dressing here. Sprinkle some olive oil on the salad (vegetable oil will do if you can't afford olive oil, but this is one thing I splurge on). Then sprinkle vinegar, salt and pepper, and a little sugar. Toss, taste, add more vinegar if necessary (lemon juice is good too), and you have an Italian dressing. For variation, you could add catsup. Now, who wants the wings? legs? and a few slices of breast. Remember, you are going to make this chicken last. With enough potatoes and salad, you don't have to eat the whole chicken.

OK, go ahead and finish the breast.

Meal two: Tomorrow, put what's left of that chicken in a pot with some chicken stock, onions, garlic, carrots, and celery and bring it to a boil, reduce, and simmer until the meat falls off the bone. You will be surprised how much meat is still left. Pour the stock through a strainer, separating the chicken from the stock, return the stock to the pot, and pick the meat off the bones. Throw the bones to the chickens, if you have chickens. It's their favorite food. They don't know it's chicken.

Set aside some of the stock. Add some of the now chopped chicken back into the soup, throw in a handful of rice or noodles, and you have chicken soup.

Meal three: Now with the rest of the meat, you can make a chicken salad or chicken enchiladas. Corn tortillas should be a staple in your fridge. Buy the big pack—it's a better deal and lasts forever if refrigerated. You can make quesadillas with them, plus chips and tostadas. You've already got a pot of beans, right? You are halfway to a Mexican meal. (See the Mexican food section for recipes with chicken in them.)

PIZZA

Talk about making your own. This is another good one for kid's parties or just to reward them if they have done their chores and homework, and if you are feeling warm and fuzzy. Start with a package of pita bread. Put out some canned marinara sauce (in a bowl--show some class!). Grate some cheese (I prefer jack). Buy whole olives and chop them yourself. (You get charged extra for sliced olives.) For more adult tastes, use chopped green peppers and onions, and bring in some of the basil and garlic from the back door garden. Let the guests build their own pizza. This works well for an inexpensive party. Though I will teach you to make your own pizza dough (see below), you can also use sliced French bread to make pizza sandwiches.

To make a real pizza, start by cooking the sauce early in the morning, as it needs to simmer for hours. This same classic red sauce works for spaghetti or any pasta. Sauté some onions (yellow is the cheapest and works just fine for almost any dish). Add garlic after the onions have turned transparent, because garlic cooks faster. Then add herbs, (fresh or dried): oregano, basil, thyme, rosemary, and a couple of bay leaves. (When you are out checking out the neighborhood for free fruit, look for a bay tree. I haven't bought bay leaves in years. I've got my favorite tree staked out and break a branch for myself every year or so. Bay is also good for any stomach ailment. Try two bay leaves in boiling water; add some honey if it's for a child. Within twenty minutes, the stomach is all better. I learned that from my old Italian housekeeper.)

Dried red chilis are cheap and last forever in a jar in the pantry. They will spice up almost everything—add just a little here. Then add canned tomato paste or sauce. The paste is concentrated and goes a lot further. It's good to keep a stock of it in the pantry, as it can be used for many things.

My secret ingredient is catsup, and if you have some red wine left over from last night (ha!), add that. Let it simmer most of the day, adding water from time to time. A couple of hours before you want the pizza, get out your baking bowl. Put in two cups of warm water (warm not hot) and add a scant of yeast, some sugar, and teaspoon salt. Let it sit until it proofs (remember that from the bread lesson?). Sift in enough flour to make a soft dough, turn it out on floured board, knead, and let it rise in the same bowl you mixed it in. (By now you have washed it and oiled it, and it is still warm.) When the dough doubles in size, punch it down, and let it rise again. You can cover it and put it in the fridge with plastic wrap over it.

When you're ready to make your pizza, knead the dough into a ball, oil a big pan, and stretch the dough in the shape you want. You can try throwing it in the air as they do in pizza parlors. Still, it's easier just to work it with oiled hands into the shape you want, round or square, thick or thin. Brush your sauce on it--not too much, or it will be soggy. Add any cheeses—the better the cheese, the better the pizza. My favorite is a three-cheese pizza. Yum! But kids don't know the difference, and plain jack will be fine.

Then add anything you want on top: bell peppers, basil,

onions, garlic, hamburger, sausage, ham, pineapple, or just herbs from the garden. And anchovies. Nobody likes anchovies except Captain Steve and me. Did you know the main ingredient in Worcestershire sauce is anchovy? And you like that, right?

CASSEROLES

Mom's special

I can't tell you how many times I heard my mother say, "What can I fix for dinner tonight that is easy and cheap?" And we knew we were going to get... "Mom's special."

Chop some onions and throw them into a cast iron skillet along with some hamburger; break it up while it's browning. When it's brown, add a can of kidney beans and a can of tomato paste, and stir in some water, salt, and pepper. Let it cook down for twenty minutes, and you've got Mom's Special. Serve with tortillas.

I was on the phone with my daughter Nancy, and I heard her tell her kids to pick up a can of kidney beans for Mom's Special. There: handed down two generations. Can't be all bad.

Tuna Janan, one of the best

Any kind of noodles, cooked

One 6-oz. can tuna (dolphin free, please)

One can cream of celery soup

½ cup mayonnaise

One cup celery, chopped (you can substitute purslane)

Half an onion, chopped

Mix everything together but the noodles and heat on a burner.

Mix in noodles and bake for twenty minutes or until it bubbles.

Add cheese or slivered almonds if you want to get fancy, but

(along with a green salad) it's a great meal as is.

Potato casserole

Four or five large potatoes, peeled and thinly sliced

One cup sour cream (or buttermilk)

One small onion chopped

One cup breadcrumbs

One cup of whatever cheese you have (jack is OK, and so is

pepper jack if you want a little oomph; cheddar is always good)

Mix everything but the potatoes (saving some breadcrumbs

for the topping), and add some fresh chopped chives, salt, and

pepper.

Of course, you make your own breadcrumbs from your homemade bread. Let the bread dry 24 hours before you make crumbs because if the bread is not dry, it will mold into another science project. Whirl it in a food processor or blender until it makes crumbs. Layer the potatoes with the gooey stuff, add the crumbs on top, and bake at 350 for 1 hour. Serve hot.

Mac and cheese

Please do not buy the boxed stuff! Read the label. If it's got things in it that you cannot pronounce, you should not be eating it. Start your macaroni in cold water, bring it to a boil, and let it simmer until not quite tender (al dente). Give it a stir and drain it in a colander, rinsing it under cold water. Grate some cheese--lots. It's OK to mix cheese—say, cheddar and jack. Mix the maraconi and cheese with milk, salt, and pepper. My grandmother uses to top hers with bacon and tomato--gorgeous. I like to add some fresh jalapenos and breadcrumbs, with butter on the top. Bake it until bubbly. Nothing can be simpler.

DINNER THE OLD-FASHIONED WAY

I cooked, the kids cleaned, we sat around a round table, and we had a conversation and played games. It was family time.

We played telephone--you know, where one person whispers something to the next, like "the corn is yellow." The next person whispers to the next, and by the time it gets to the last person, they say it out loud, and it is not even close to what the first person said.

This game develops into a full conversation about how people don't communicate. What you think you heard is not what they meant to say. It's a good game. Sometimes we would have manners contests--me, of course, being the judge--and the winner did not have to do the dishes. Nancy was good at the manners contest. Another game is called "I'm going on a trip." It goes like this: "I'm going on a trip, and I'm taking a suitcase." The next person repeats and says, "I'm going on a trip, and I'm taking a suitcase and a toothbrush." The third person repeats "I'm going on a trip, and I'm taking a suitcase and a toothbrush and an elephant"—the fourth person same thing, adding striped pajamas. Fifth, now you gotta repeat everything and add your suitcase, toothbrush, elephant, striped pajamas, etc. It can go on for a long time when you start taking weird things--it gets more interesting. I think the record, held by Monah, is sixteen things. Dinner happened at a round table that had a warp in it. If you put a plate at that point, it would slide into your lap—a favorite place to put guests, always good for a laugh.

SALADS

Caesar salad 101

Chicken does not belong in a Caesar salad when it's made right. This is a whole meal. Serve with crusty french bread in a wooden bowl, if you are lucky enough to own one. Again, look in thrift stores.

Serves 6 (unless Phil is at the table--then he'll eat it all)
2 cloves garlic
2 anchovy fillets mashed together
1 tbsp. Grey Poupon mustard
Heavy dash of Worcestershire sauce
1 dash Tabasco
Juice of one lemon and equal amount of olive oil
2 heads of romaine lettuce
Croutons

Crush the garlic with a pestle and add the anchovies (yes, anchovies, get over it. It's what makes a Caesar salad.) Mash them together. Now the Grey Poupon mustard. Yes, I know it's expensive. But a little goes a long way, and it's worth it. Add a splash of Worcestershire, and mix it all together. Now squeeze the juice of one lemon and add equal parts of olive oil. None of this can be substituted, so if you don't have the ingredients, don't make it. Hot-dog mustard won't do, and neither will vegetable oil.

However, you can make your own croutons, and they will be better than packaged ones. Cut your French bread into little squares and toast them in the oven with a bit of oil. You can add herbs, but it's not necessary, because the salad dressing carries the salad. So, tear (do not chop) a head of romaine, add it to the bowl's dressing, and throw in the croutons. Add salt and pepper (preferably freshly ground pepper), and toss with some grated asiago cheese or parmesan. Serve immediately. This is the real deal that you will get only in fancy restaurants where the salad is made at the table with a flourish.

Do not buy bottled dressing. It's for lazy people, full of preservatives, and expensive. For the price of the bottled dressing, you can make a whole salad.

Green salad

The greener the lettuce, the better. Forget iceberg, or mix it with healthier greens—spinach, kale, purslane. The basis of a green salad is lettuce, and then you can add anything: vegetables sliced thin, tomatoes for color, black olives (stock up when they are on sale; the small ones are better in a salad). Red onion, grated carrots, green onion, and peas (fresh or frozen), or a combination of any three will do, or just lettuce. My friend Sher puts berries in her salads. The trick is in the dressing. The easiest is after your choice of vegetables are in a pretty bowl. Food tastes better when it looks good. Splash some olive oil on it. Vegetable oil will do if you don't have olive oil—some vinegar, preferably red, a dash of sugar, salt, and pepper. If you are going to make a south-of-the-border salad, add a can of beans, rinsed and drained, and corn and chopped cilantro. Add a teaspoon of cumin—this goes great with tacos, tamale pies, or enchiladas.

Crunchy salad

Mix bite-size florets of cauliflower and broccoli, and celery. Add frozen peas just before serving (they defrost quickly). Add peanuts. Serve with ranch dressing. (I make my own. It's less expensive than the bottled stuff and better because it has no preservatives.)

Ranch dressing

Dry mix (makes about 8 cups; keep in a mason jar and use as needed)

1 1/2 tablespoons dill

2 teaspoons dried parsley

1 teaspoon garlic powder

½ teaspoon onion powder

1 teaspoon black pepper

1 teaspoon salt

Dressing (2 cups):

In a mixing bowl, combine 2 tablespoons dry mix, 1 cup mayonnaise, and 1 cup buttermilk (if you don't have buttermilk, add a tablespoon of white vinegar to a cup of milk and let it sit for five minutes). Mix it all together and refrigerate, covered, for 24 hours, to let the flavors blend.

Potato salad

This can be made in many ways. When I lived in San Francisco, my roommate Maxine could go into the kitchen when there

was nothing to eat and make something out of nothing--
potato salad was one of those things. In the Fillmore, hot links
and potato salad was served in most eateries. Instead of big
chunks of half-cooked potato, the potatoes were cooked till
they were falling apart. The salad was almost like mashed
potatoes—with mayonnaise the key ingredient and then
mustard. If you had pickle relish or pickles, you could chop
them in. Add any color onions, chopped fine. If you have hard-
boiled eggs, grate them into the salad, add salt and pepper,
and you have your basic potato salad. You can substitute
vinaigrette for the mayonnaise. Try adding celery. Bacon is
great in a potato salad, and so is blue cheese. But the basic is
best for kids. Make it ahead of time and let the flavors merge.
Or on a winter night, serve hot potato salad, German-style; use
the vinaigrette and leave out the eggs. Serve with hot dogs or
sausage.

Three-bean salad (a good summer salad)
Open and rinse three cans of beans, one each of kidney, white,
and green beans (sliced thin, French cut).
Mix these with a can of small black olives, a whole red onion
thinly sliced, and one bell pepper, chopped. Now go out into
the garden and cut some basil with your scissors.

To this, add

1/3 cup red wine vinegar

1/3 cup sugar

1/2 cup oil

¼ tsp. garlic powder

Some salad herbs

Mix it all together, cover, and refrigerate several hours or overnight. It's great to take to barbecues.

Regular coleslaw

Chop one head of cabbage and grate four carrots. Add vinegar--any kind will do, but I like seasoned rice vinegar--salt and pepper, and sugar. Now, if you like Kentucky Fried Chicken coleslaw, add *a cup* of sugar. Yeah, that's why the kids like it; it's got a lot of sugar in it. But make your slaw your own by tasting and adding vinegar and sugar as you see fit.

Crunchy slaw

Sliver thinly (matchstick-size) three carrots, one cucumber, and one bell pepper. Add one bunch of scallions (green onions), ½ cup cilantro leaves from your pot garden, and a handful of peanuts, slightly chopped.

In another bowl, mix two tbsp. peanut butter, 2 tsp. fresh grated ginger, 2 tsp. rice wine vinegar, 1 tbsp. oil (canola if you have it), and 2 tbsp. sesame oil. (It's expensive, but a little goes a long way.) Add the juice of two or three limes, depending on their size. Mix together and toss over salad—it's my current favorite.

Poor man's salad dressing

Let's not throw out the dregs of mayonnaise. catsup, and mustard jars that are stored in the rear of the refrigerator. When enough jars are available, rinse each with a little wine vinegar. Pour the rinsings into the mayonnaise jar with a bit of leftover wine (ha!). Add salt and pepper, and shake well until the dressing is smooth, light pink in color, and a delight to taste.

Thai chicken salad

For the dressing:

¼ cup rice wine vinegar

1 tbsp. minced fresh ginger

¼ cup honey (I use less because I don't like it too sweet)

Pinch cayenne

One tbsp. hot chile oil

1 tbsp. sesame oil (I use 2 because I like it}

1 tbsp. soy sauce

1 tsp. minced French garlic

Put all in a small Cuisinart (I got mine at a thrift store for $3) and blend.

For the salad:

One head of romaine or any green lettuce

One chicken breast, boiled (use the stock for soup later; throw in some celery, onions, and carrots)

One can mandarin oranges

One package top ramen or rice noodles

One bunch of green onions

Shred or chop the chicken. Cook, rinse, and drain the noodles, and let cool. (Put them in the freezer if you're in a hurry.)

Toss the noodles with the dressing and add the rest of the ingredients. Throw in a handful of chopped peanuts at the end. My family loves this salad, and it's a full meal, especially in summer.

MEAT

I do not eat red meat much unless it is organic or at least grass-fed. If I am invited to someone's home and do not want to insult my host, I will eat a small portion or hide it in my napkin. Still, for those of you who cannot live without it, some cheap cuts have more flavor than others and, when correctly prepared, are very good.

Chuck steak is one of them. I ate a lot of it when I was in college. You can have the butcher cut a roast to about two inches thick. The bone is the best part—the closer the bone, the sweeter the meat. And if you don't want to gnaw on the bone, save it for the minestrone soup.

Rub it with garlic and sear it in a hot cast iron pan (if you don't have one by now, you are not listening to me) until brown.

Hamburger

There are so many things to do with hamburger besides the classic hamburger. For years I would bread and fry eggplant and serve it to my kids as hamburger once the sandwich was assembled with pickle, mustard, mayo, catsup, lettuce, tomato, and onions. It tasted like a hamburger and was better for them. One day, my son Beau did the unthinkable--he lifted off the bun and shouted, "this is not a hamburger!" The other children did likewise, and that was the last time I got away with feeding them a healthy alternative.

Back to hamburger. The best meatloaf is made with equal parts sausage and hamburger. As my friend Sher says, put everything in the fridge into it. Onions, of course, garlic, celery, carrots, olives, a handful of herbs, parsley, rosemary, oregano, thyme, fennel, basil, whatever you have growing in your windowsill or out the back door. Add something for filler, either breadcrumbs or a cup of oatmeal. Get a couple of eggs, a can of tomato paste or sauce, mash it all together in a big bowl with your hands, and form it into a meatloaf. Sometimes I rinse out the catsup bottle and add that. Cheese is good too but not necessary. Put it in a pan in the oven for about an hour and before taking it out, pour a little tomato sauce mixed with a bit of Worcestershire and a dash of Tabasco sauce over the middle of the meatloaf and cook for another five minutes. Serve with potatoes that have been peeled, quartered, and baked in the same pan with the meatloaf. You need to turn them a couple of times with a fork, and if the meatloaf is particularly lean, you need to coat them with oil.

Sometimes I put the meat on low and cook overnight. Then I serve it in a bowl with rice and beans, or make burritos out of it for the next meal, saving enough of the sauce to pour over it. A wet burrito is better than a dry one. To make a burrito, put some day-old rice and beans in a tortilla, spoon in the salsa verde, and roll it up. Add some cheese on top of the wet burrito and put it in the oven at 450 for ten minutes or until the cheese melts.

You can make it in a food processor, but if you don't have one, you can hand-chop everything. (It takes a while longer, but if you don't have a food processor, you probably have all day anyway.)

Pulled pork

To make pulled pork, slice the pork instead of cubing it. Before it finishes cooking, add your favorite barbecue sauce and let it cook an extra hour. Pull a fork thru it to break it up and serve it on hamburger buns or your own french bread with coleslaw (see the Salads section).

MASHED POTATOES

Cut your potatoes into small pieces. That way, they cook faster and save energy. The secret to good mashed potatoes is to mash the hell of them, making sure you go to the bottom of the pan and scrape the sides with the masher, and adding butter and cream. Half and half will do; so will skin milk. Just about everything tastes better with butter and cream, salt, and white pepper (o one wants black specks in their mashed potatoes). Then here's the secret: whip them with a silver fork after you have mashed them. For some reason, it makes them whiter and fluffier. If you don't have Grandma's silver, buy a silver fork at a thrift store.

Speaking of forks, did you know that if you put a fork in an open bottle of champagne, it would keep it bubbly for several days? I don't know why, I just know it works.

ETHNIC FOOD

Seventy-five percent of the world lives on rice, beans, and vegetables. It's healthier than fast food. When I was in Thailand, there were no fat people, and everyone ate all the time. But it was fish, vegetables, rice, and everything tasted great.

I brought back three cookbooks. The key is freshness, and vegetables and fish steamed rather than deep-fried. It's the sauces: soy sauce, ginger, garlic, chili peppers, fish sauce, lemon or lime juice.

A basic soup is chicken stock with all the above in it. Then you can add chicken, beef, or fish. And of course, noodles. Thin rice noodles are the best. Chop up any fresh vegetables you have and add them to the top of the soup before serving. Play with this soup, adding more or less to taste. But go easy on the fish sauce; it's powerful, a little goes a long way. A bottle will last you for months, if not years.

Indian food

For a cheap and easy-to-make appetizer, try Hummus.

Hummus

One can garbanzo beans with fluid

One lemon, squeezed

Two cloves garlic

Blend these in a food processor and salt to taste. Refrigerate for a few hours or overnight. Pour onto a plate. With a spoon, make an indenture in the middle and pour in a little olive oil. Serve with flatbread for dipping or crudités (raw vegetables, you philistine!).

Flatbread or chapati
2 cups flour, preferably whole wheat
4 tsp. butter
2/3 cup water
Salt

Sift the flour and salt into a large bowl. Add the butter and rub it into the flour. Make a well in the center and pour in water a little at a time, mixing with your fingers. Form the dough into a ball and transfer it to a floured board. Knead for about 10 minutes or until elastic. Put the dough in a bowl, cover, and set aside at room temperature for 30 minutes. Divide it into eight portions and roll out each portion into a round shape. Heat a cast iron pan to medium-hot. Put one portion of dough into the pan; when small blisters appear, press to flatten it. Turn it over and cook until pale golden. Remove from pan and put in a clean napkin to serve. You can embellish this with melted butter and slightly toasted garlic.

Basic curry

You can make curry many ways with vegetables--potato curry, for instance. You can buy curry powder or create your own.

In vegetable oil, saute four sliced or chopped yellow onions, ginger, garlic, two apples, and six chopped garlic cloves for three to five minutes. Add spices: 2 tablespoons turmeric, 2 tablespoons coriander, mustard seed, one or two jalapenos, and cumin seeds. Add four cups chicken stock. Add four cups of chicken or turkey (or potatoes cut in chunks if you're vegetarian). Simmer for two hours at least, adding water to cover and then a can of coconut milk. This curry is better the second day.

Condiments:
Major Grey's chutney
Chopped green onions
Chopped hard-boiled egg
Shredded coconut
Chopped bananas
Chopped raisins

Curry can be hot if you want; add chili peppers, fresh or dried.

You can make it with any vegetables--cauliflower is a favorite in India.

Dal soup (spiced lentil soup)
1 tsp. clarified butter

1 onion

1 garlic clove, crushed

1 green chili

1 tsp. ground cinnamon

½ tsp. hot chili powder

1 cup dried lentils, washed and drained

3 cups of water

1/2 tsp. salt

1 cup coconut milk (optional; if you don't have any, add more water)

Melt the butter, add the onions and garlic, and sauté. Add the spices and lentils and pour in the water. Add the salt, bring to a boil, and then turn the heat down and simmer for about thirty minutes. Puree this in a blender--it merges the spices more. This is a fast, easy soup, and you can change the seasonings by adding curry powder or paprika, whatever is available. Serve hot.

Vindaloo

You can use chicken or pork. Traditionally, beef is not used in India.

2 lbs. chicken, pork, or vegetables

2 cups stock

2-in. piece of fresh green ginger, peeled, or the old dried-out stuff you get in stores

4 garlic cloves, chopped

1 1/2 tsp. hot chili powder

2 tsp. turmeric (you can buy turmeric in bulk at ethnic stores for very little money. It's very good for you, and you can use it in lots of other dishes besides Indian ones, not to mention tea)

2 tbsp. coriander seeds (another bulk buy--very cheap and lasts forever)

2 tsp. cardamom seeds

6 whole cloves

6 peppercorns

1 cinnamon stick (buy in bulk)

1 tsp. cumin seeds (buy in bulk)

2/3 cup vinegar

4 bay leaves

3 tbsp. vegetable oil

1 tsp. mustard seeds

2/3 cup water

1 tsp. salt

Put the spices and vinegar into a blender and blend until smooth, adding more liquid if necessary. Put the cubed meat into a large bowl and stir in the spice paste. Cover and set aside to marinate at room temperature for 1 hour. Lay the bay leaves on top, cover, and chill in the fridge overnight, turning from time to time.

Two hours before dinner, heat oil in a pan (preferably cast iron). Add mustard seeds, cover the pan, and fry the seeds until they spatter. Add the meat-and-spice mixture, bring to a boil, and simmer for 40 minutes, covered. If needed, add more water, stir, and simmer for another 30 minutes.

Serve with rice. I like basmati brown rice, but any rice you have will do. It's delicious and worth taking the time for.

Mango chutney

Served with curry, chutney adds that extra oomph. Major Grey's is excellent but very expensive. You can make your own. Here's one recipe, though I'm still looking for a better one. If you find one, tell me.

3 lbs. mangos, peeled and chopped

¾ cup of salt

2 cups sugar

2 1/2 cups white wine vinegar

2-inch piece of green ginger, peeled

6 garlic cloves, crushed

2 tsp. hot chili powder

1 cinnamon stick

1 cup pitted dates

2/3 cup raisins

Chop the mangos finely and put in a bowl. Add the salt and about 8 cups water. Cover and let sit for 24 hours.

Put the sugar and vinegar into a saucepan and bring it to boil, stirring until the sugar has dissolved. Stir in the mangos, add the rest of the ingredients, and bring to a boil, occasionally stirring. Reduce the heat to low and simmer for about an hour and a half until the chutney is very thick. Remove the cinnamon stick and ladle the chutney into warm jars. You should have enough to last you for a while.

Middle Eastern food

Falafel

My Arab friend taught me to make falafel, which are good wrapped in flatbread.

1 lb. dried garbanzos, soaked overnight in warm water

2 onions, white or yellow

1 tsp. cumin

1 tsp. cayenne

Salt and pepper

2 cloves garlic

1 lemon

1 tsp. each parsley and mint leaves, chopped

1/4 cup water

3 tbsp. tahini

Drain the beans and put them and everything else in a food processor. Form into balls the size of a walnut and drop into hot oil. Yeah, deep-fried, but they are delicious drizzled with yogurt, lime, and cumin sauce.

Mexican food

Beans and rice

Buy bulk pinto beans (30 pounds under 20 dollars at most ethnic stores). It's the same with rice; you can feed a family for six months on rice and beans.

You no longer have to soak the beans overnight. Cover the beans with cold water and put on the back of the stove. Bring to a boil, and then let them simmer for two hours, adding chopped onion and garlic. Never add salt until they are finished cooking.

If you are making bean soup, add oregano, cumin, and whatever greens you have around (kale, spinach, chard, purslane) plus carrots. If you make whole Mexican beans, just the oregano, cumin, onion, and garlic will do.

Why are beans called "refried?" They're not fried again; they're just smashed or mashed with a potato masher.

To make Mexican rice, start with the cast iron pan and add some oil or lard.
(Lard is not as bad as you think; it's better than margarine and makes the best piecrust. Don't tell my daughter Chinarose that I use lard in my lemon meringue pie crust; she thinks my pie is the best.) Then add chopped onions and garlic, 1 1/2 cup grated carrots, and a can of tomato sauce or paste. I usually mix it with a cup of water. When the onions and garlic are sautéed, pour in the water and cover, and cook for 20 minutes until you see little holes in the mixture. It's done. Many Mexican cooks add peas. I add frozen peas at the end, fluffing them into the rice.

Fiesta soup

This is a pretty soup, and we could make it very quickly when we ran out of soup at the restaurant.

1 quart chicken stock

1 large onion

2 cloves garlic

1 zucchini

1 carrot

1 red bell pepper

Fresh corn from the cob

1 can of white beans

Salt

Pepper

Topping

1 small bunch cilantro

1 jalapeno pepper

1 tomato

This soup will serve four people. You can double it to serve eight or double it again for sixteen or more. Chop all vegetables into small pieces. Bring the chicken stock to a boil. Add vegetables, simmer 20 minutes, remove from heat, and garnish with chopped cilantro, jalapenos, and tomatoes.

Tortilla soup

This is a favorite at most Mexican restaurants. Timing is everything—it must be served pronto.

2 quarts chicken stock

One or two cups cooked chicken, shredded

½ cup of cilantro

2 chopped tomatoes

1 white or yellow onion, sliced thin

1 tsp. chili flakes (optional)

Salt and pepper

For the chicken: you can use the leftovers after roasting a chicken. Put the carcass in cold water with one chopped onion and some chopped garlic. Bring it to a boil and let it simmer till the meat pulls off the bone. Take out the carcass, use a fork to strip off the meat, and put it in the broth. You can also use boneless chicken thighs or breasts; cover them with water and bring to a boil, simmer until white, cut the meat into small strips, and add to the broth.

Add the other ingredients.

Toppings:

4 cups corn tortilla strips (cut in 1-inch strips and fried in oil until crispy)

1 cup chopped cilantro

2 cups grated sharp cheddar

2 ripe avocados, chopped

Have all garnishes in bowls (except for the avocado) ready to go. Pour the soup into individual soup bowls while it's piping hot; then add the toppings. Serve at once, so the chips do not get soggy. Delicious.

Garlic soup

2 cups of chicken stock

4 to 6 heads of garlic, depending on the size

1 tbsp. ground black pepper

1 tbsp. white pepper

1 quart heavy cream or half-and-half, depending on your health

¼ cup butter

¼ cup flour, sifted

Salt to taste

To make the roux, melt the butter in a pan, add the flour, and mix till firm. Take it out of the pan and store till needed.

Mince garlic finely. Put it in a cast-iron skillet. Add butter, heat until it melts, and add the roux, chicken stock, and cream. Do not bring to boil; simmer 10-20 minutes. Taste the soup and add pepper and salt to taste. Be careful not to burn the soup. It must be creamy and thick enough to be soup. It's terrific if you get it right. Pay attention. Do not answer the phone when you are making this soup. Serve with a garnish of cheese and cilantro.

Tortillas

Buy them when they are cheap. I have never mastered making them and never tried. The store-bought ones last forever in the fridge. And what is Mexican food without chips?

It's much better to make your own; they are fresh and hot and go with everything. Since writing this, I have been making my own chips in a deep fryer or a large pot of very hot oil. Cut tortillas into any shape you like, and fry till golden brown. Salt immediately. (Speaking of deep-frying: next time you peel the potatoes for mashed potatoes, don't throw away the peels. Deep-fry them 'til they're crispy, salt them, and enjoy—they're cheaper than potato chips and have no preservatives.

Salsa

Many people have said my salsa is the best they have ever tasted. Maybe they are just nice, or perhaps it is the best salsa ever. I think so.

Chop one red onion (my preference, but any onion will do). Chop and add one large or two small chili peppers. They are easy to grow and take very little room on a windowsill or just outside the back door. Jalapenos are good, or serranos will do, but watch out for habaneros or thai peppers; they are *very* hot and will scald the taste buds right off your tongue. Add some cilantro if you have it, and a can of crushed tomatoes. (Any can of tomatoes will do cause they are going to be crushed anyway. Buy what's on sale.) If you have fresh tomatoes starting to go soft, use them instead. Add salt and pepper to taste, and then you have salsa that can go in the beans or be served with chips.

Tacos

Real tacos served in Mexico are made of corn tortillas with chicken or beef or pork—or even linga (tongue). They are excellent with chilies or hot sauce, nothing more. A taco stand in Mexico offers ten different sauces or salsas with their tacos. But here in U.S., we are used to Gringo tacos with lettuce and cheese. For you busy mothers, here's a Gringo taco recipe:

1 lb. hamburger or ground turkey

1 large onion

1 clove garlic

1 tbsp. taco seasoning

1 lb. corn tortillas

Fry the hamburger with chopped onions and garlic and taco seasoning.

If you don't have taco seasoning, make some.

Taco seasoning

1 tbsp. each:

Chile powder

Cumin

Oregano

Onion powder

Garlic powder, cayenne, paprika

If you have a gas stove, put the tortilla on the flame for a few seconds and flip to heat both sides. If you have an electric stove, put the tortilla in a very hot pan for a few seconds and flip. Fill the tortilla and serve with lettuce and cheese, just like Taco Bell. Don't buy taco sauce with MSG--make my salsa instead, but leave out the peppers if you're serving to children.

Tostadas

Tostadas were my first introduction to Mexican food at a Mexican birthday party. I thought it was the best thing I had ever eaten—it probably was at that point. My mother was one of the worst cooks ever. Really! She was always trying recipes out of *Better Homes and Gardens*, and they never came out right. She would look at the picture and look at her concoction and say, I don't understand. Then she would go back to serving her regular meals, consisting of some sort of meat burned to a crisp, lumpy mashed potatoes, and canned vegetables dumped out of the can into a pan. The vegetables were warmed and poured into a bowl and put on the table--no seasoning, nothing, just icky canned beans or spinach.

Back to tostadas. Use corn tortillas. They are cheaper and better for you. Bake or deep-fry them till crisp. Take part of the beans off the stove and mash them with a potato masher (electric or old-fashioned). These are not refried beans, not fried at all, just mashed and I don't know why they are called refried. Google it!

Smear the beans on the crisp tortilla, and you have a tostada. Little kids like just bean and cheese. I like them fully loaded-- beans, grated cheese, chopped lettuce, salsa, and if you have cilantro, that too. If you are feeling good about it, you can add chicken, cooked and shredded.

Enchiladas

Remember the third-day chicken? Buy a can of green chili salsa and make enchiladas. Fill the tortillas with cheese and a little chopped onion; roll them up and place them in a baking dish. You can add chicken to this, or you can do just cheese and some chicken. Soften the tortillas first by dipping them in the canned sauce—or, if you have a gas stove, hold them over the flames, turn, and voila, you got soft tortillas.

Ceviche

You can also make ceviche by taking any white fish, chopping it, marinating it in lime juice, and adding chopped onion, tomatoes, and cilantro. The lime cooks the fish, so you need to marinate it for at least an hour.

Shrimp can be used instead of fish, but it's usually more expensive. Never use canned shrimp. Get it from the fish market, freh, or buy it frozen. Tostadas are fun. You can put out the fixings and let kids or adults make their own.

Mexican casserole

½ cup sliced celery

1/2 cup chopped onion

3 cups cooked beans, including the water they are cooked in

1 cup canned corn

1 lb. hamburger

Sauté onions, garlic, and celery in a little oil--or if the hamburger is fatty, just add the hamburger to the vegetables and and brown them together. Add Mexican seasoning: oregano, chili powder, cumin. Mix it all, layer it with corn tortillas cut into triangles, and sprinkle with cheese.

Now this is not much different from a tamale pie. Try the recipe on the back of the yellow cornmeal box. It's about as good as it gets, same with the cornbread.

My friend Kelly makes the best cornbread. He puts more sugar in it and eggs, and gets higher, lighter cornbread. I like to make it in a cast iron skillet and serve it on in the skillet. Cornbread goes good with pork. Always shop the sales; buy whatever is on sale. Whether it's pork or chicken, one of them will be on special that week, and with pork, you can make chili verde or pulled-pork sandwiches. If you have a crockpot, use that or a large pot.

Chili verde

Buy the cheapest cut of pork you can get. Cut it into bite-size pieces and put it in the crockpot with two chopped onions and a handful of garlic. If you are using a regular pot, brown it first; if you're using a crockpot, just throw it in there. Peel and cut the tomatillos and add them to the meat with a can or bottle of beer (this makes the meat very tender). Tomatillos are cheap at Mexican markets. Pick the largest ones you can get. Peel the parchment-like skin off, cut in half, and throw them in the pot (about equal parts pork and tomatillos). Add a couple of jalapenos if you like it spicy, add enough water to cover it all, and let it cook for about four hours.

These are the easy Mexican dishes. If you want to go further, check the internet, or get a Mexican cookbook.

Chili Verde

5 cups diced onion

1/2 cup chopped garlic

1/2 cup chopped serrano or jalapeno peppers

1 quart chicken broth

12 anaheim peppers

2 lbs. tomatillos

1 can beer

1 tsp. chili powder

3 tbsp. garlic powder

1 tbsp. ground cumin

1 tbsp. Mexican oregano

1 tsp. ground coriander

½ cup corn flour to thicken

Salt and pepper

Soul food

If you don't think this is ethnic food, you have never lived in the Fillmore. I will not give you the recipe for chitlins; they are gross and disgusting. When I went into my Afro American friend's house, it smelled so funky, and I would say, "What is the terrible smell?" She would grin ear to ear and say, "chitlins." It's cows' stomach no matter how you look at it. I have eaten heart, brain, tongue, and liver--all have their merits. Still, I can not stomach cow stomach. But she made delicious cornbread and ribs. Here is her recipe.

Cornbread

1 cup yellow cornmeal

1 cup flour

½ sugar

1 tsp. baking powder

1 tsp. salt

1 cup buttermilk (to make buttermilk, put 1 tsp. white vinegar in milk)

½ cup vegetable oil

1 large egg, beaten

Mix sugar and oil and then egg and milk. Add all dry ingredients, mix well, and pour into a 9-inch baking pan. Bake at 350 until a toothpick comes out clean. Serve hot with butter and honey.

Maxine's ribs
Sauce:

½ cup onions, minced

1 tsp. oil or butter

½ cup water

2 tsp. vinegar

1 tsp. Worcestershire sauce

Juice of one lemon

2 tsp. mustard

½ cup chili sauce

Hot sauce to taste (Maxine made it hot)

Salt and pepper

Sauté the onions in oil. Add the remaining ingredients and simmer for 15 minutes. Adjust seasoning to taste, and if you have any whiskey, put it in.

Ribs:

Maxine said to steam the ribs beforehand. It makes it possible to char the outside quickly without leaving the inside raw and keeps the meat from shrinking. Place the ribs in a baking pan on a rack and pour water in the bottom of the pan, making sure that the ribs do not rest in the water. Cover the baking pan tightly and place it in the oven at 250 for two hours. Turn it once. Each side should be steamed, so the meat is no longer pink. When it's cool, apply barbeque sauce lavishly, and cook ribs quickly or in a very hot oven for 10 minutes. Finger-lickin' good.

Collard greens

I got this recipe in New Orleans at a place called Ajax--the best.

1 bunch kale

1 bunch spinach

1 bunch chard (or you can mix this up using beet tops, dandelion greens, or mustard greens)

1 lb. bacon (½ lb. will do, but I like bacon)

1 large yellow onion

¼ cup seasoned rice vinegar

Salt and pepper

Fry the bacon until crispy, take out, and chop. Sauté the onions in the bacon drippings (maybe take out some of it—you don't want it greasy), and then add the greens till they are just limp. Sprinkle with the vinegar, add the bacon, salt and pepper to taste, and serve.

Southern salad

2 cups canned or cooked black-eyed peas

1 cup celery

1 cup diced tomatoes

1 red onion, sliced very thin

Mayonnaise to taste

Add celery, tomatoes, and mayonnaise to the peas. Toss lightly and garnish with the onion.

Hush puppies

Loved by children, old men, and dogs.

2 cups cornmeal

2 tsp. baking powder

1 tsp. salt

1 1/2 cups milk

1 large onion, chopped fine

Sift the dry ingredients together and add the milk. Stir in the chopped onion. Add more cornmeal or milk as necessary to form a soft but workable dough. With your hands, make pieces of the dough into pones (oblong cakes, about 5 inches long and 3 inches wide). Fry in hot deep fat until well-browned. Serve with catfish.

Blackened catfish

While in Corpus Christi, Texas, I stopped at an oyster house and had the best blackened catfish I have ever had. I waited two hours until the chef was free to get this recipe. I told him, "Do not leave anything out, and I will give you a dessert recipe that will be a best seller." (That recipe is in the dessert section.)

2 oz. cayenne pepper

2 oz. black pepper

2 oz. white pepper

4 oz. onion powder

6 oz. garlic powder

2 oz. basil

2 oz. thyme

2 oz. oregano

2 oz. bay leaf, ground

Pinch of salt

Pinch of sugar

Grind all spices until they are the consistency of a spice rub. Rub all over fish, cover both sides, and fry in an iron skillet with a little olive oil.

Italian food

What's the sound spaghetti makes when it hits the wall? WHOP!

Start with an antipasto. When I was in Pennsylvania in the middle of nowhere, looking for a good restaurant in a two-horse town, the only place that looked good was an Italian restaurant. But when they served me the antipasto, it consisted of a whole tomato, a bunch of celery with the store wrapper still on, and some radishes with the tops and bottoms on them. I started looking for the hidden camera, thinking it was a joke. It was, but no camera.

It just goes to prove that an antipasto can be anything—an

excellent time to clean the refrigerator. Make a plate of pickles, olives, hard-boiled eggs, salami radishes, artichoke hearts, celery, cheeses, any sausage you may have, and crostini.

Toast some bread, preferably French, and brush it with olive oil. Anything can go on top: tomato, anchovies, that can of sardines in the back of the cupboard. Then serve on a large platter, Italian style.

But if you have the ingredients and time, here is a real antipasto recipe.

Antipasto

1 cup each catsup, tomato-based chili sauce, and water

½ cup each olive oil, tarragon wine vinegar, and lemon juice

1 clove garlic, minced

2 tbsp. firmly packed brown sugar

1 tbsp. each Worcestershire sauce and prepared horseradish

½ cauliflower

3 medium-sized carrots

2 stalks celery

½ pound small whole mushrooms

1 jar pepperoni

2 cans solid-pack tuna

1 can rolled anchovies with capers

Pimiento-stuffed Spanish-style olives

Dash cayenne pepper

In a large saucepan, combine the catsup, chile sauce, water, oil, vinegar, lemon juice, garlic, brown sugar, Worcestershire, horseradish, and cayenne. Bring to a boil and simmer for a few minutes. Cut the cauliflower into florets. Peel the carrots and slice into ¼ inch pieces (use a ruffle-edged cutter if you have one). Slice the celery diagonally into 1 ¼-inch pieces. Add to the sauce the cauliflower, carrots, celery, mushrooms, and pepperoncini. Cover and simmer slowly for 20 minutes or until tender-crisp. Drain tuna and add it, taking care to keep pieces as whole as possible. Simmer just until heated. Cool, refrigerate overnight, and serve on a platter.

Pasta

Pasta dishes can be as simple as spaghetti with olive oil and roasted garlic, or as complicated as lasagne.

Pasta sauce

In a cast iron skillet, sauté 1 large yellow onion and 4 minced garlic cloves.

Add the following:

1 large can of crushed tomatoes or four small cans of tomato

paste or sauce

1 bay leaf

1 tsp. oregano, preferably fresh

1 tsp. rosemary, ditto

1 tsp. thyme, ditto

6 tbsp. fennel

Salt and pepper

Catsup (f you have a half-empty bottle of catsup, fill it with

water, shake it, and dump it in; it's my secret ingredient)

Simmer this for two hours, adding water when needed or some

of that leftover red wine. You can add meat with the onions

and garlic, but this is your basic pasta sauce and is fine without.

All kids love it. Put it on spaghetti, fettuccini, egg noodles,

whatever you have in the pantry. Serve with a green salad, and

you have an Italian meal.

Pasta puttanesca

This is a Martha Stewart recipe that I have converted. It's easy

to make in a few moments. "Puttanesca" means prostitute.

These women were in a hurry to eat and get to work.

Coarse salt

1 lb. spaghetti or linguine

3 tbsp. olive oil

6 medium cloves garlic, minced

10 anchovies, crushed (sometimes I substitute two cans of clams)

1 can Italian plum tomatoes, chopped and strained (save the juice)

1 tbsp. capers

½ cup kalamata olives, pitted and coarsely chopped

2 tbsp. coarsely chopped fresh parsley

In a large pot of boiling water, cook pasta for about ten minutes. Drain. While the pasta is cooking, heat oil in a large skillet, add the garlic, red pepper flakes, and anchovies, and cook (stirring) 1 to 2 minutes. Add drained tomatoes, capers, the tomato juice, and olives. Bring to a boil and lower heat to keep at a simmer, frequently stirring until slightly thickened, about 5 minutes. Stir the pasta into the sauce, sprinkle parsley on top, serve immediately, and get back to work.

FREE MEAT

If you live in the city, this does not apply to you. Well maybe it does, if you have pigeons. Young pigeons are called squab and are served in fancy French restaurants. If you can kill and dress a chicken, you can dress a pigeon. Or a rabbit, possum, raccoon, or rat, for that matter. Yes, people do survive on all of them, though there is little meat on a raccoon (or a cat). But if you are hungry enough, you will eat them.

When a deer jumped in front of my Datsun, I had no choice. It committed suicide using my car. I got out of the car, held its head while it took its last breath, said a prayer for it, and then hoisted it into the trunk of the car.

I went home and called Uncle Donald, who came and hung the deer. It's essential to hang it outside, and have a hose ready, because it's a messy job. You slit its throat and drain the blood. Take a four-inch sharp knife and run it down from throat to tail, taking out the internal organs (but save the liver and kidney). Drop the organs into a large bucket. If this does not make you a vegetarian, now you must skin the poor thing. Start at the neck, make an incision, and slice, trying not to injure the meat. Yes, it's meat now, not Bambi. Oh, I forgot, it's easier if you cut off its legs and arms first. Oh, I mean legs.
Keep the meat cool and let it hang.

Now it's time for the hard part--butchering the damn thing. I was up all night with a hack saw. It reminded me of Alfred Hitchcock's movie, *Rear window*. Get some butcher paper and sharp knives. Wrap the dismembered (used to be living) thing, and put it in your freezer. Here is my venison recipe. It has turned vegetarians into carnivores. They only saw the result--a lovely piece of roasted meat.

Marinade for 70 lb of venison
½ gallon oil
6 bottles catsup

1 qt. apple cider vinegar

1 small bottle mustard

3 small bottles horseradish

½ bottle Italian dressing

Dash mace

6 drops Worcestershire sauce

2 heads garlic

Three bottles of catsup water

Mix it all up, put the venison in a large container, add the marinade, and marinate overnight. Roasting it on a spit on a fall evening is great fun. Gather around the campfire, with a bottle or two.

Stuffed possum

When I was ten, I found a baby possum in the woods while I was "exploring." I brought it home and kept it as a pet. Herman was very sweet but nocturnal, and I will never forget my mother's scream when she found him under her pillow. I did not eat him, but if you are a survivalist, they are edible.

1 dressed possum

1 cup salt

1 large onion

1 cup breadcrumbs

Worcestershire sauce

1 egg, hard-boiled

To dress a possum, remove the entrails, head, and tail (save the tail to pick your teeth with later). And of course, the skin. It's a pretty silver-gray; you can make a hand muff out of it. Wash thoroughly inside and out. Save the liver. Cover with water and about 1 cup salt. Let stand overnight. In the morning, drain it and rinse well with clear boiling water.

To make the stuffing, melt some butter in a pan and add the chopped onion. When the onion begins to brown, add finely chopped liver. Cook until the liver is well done. Add breadcrumbs, red pepper, and a dash of Worcestershire sauce. Mix in a chopped hard-boiled egg. Salt the stuffing, and add water to moisten. Stuff the possum with the mix and sew the ends closed. Add some water to a roasting pan and put the possum in. Roast until tender and browned, basting it in its own fat. Serve with yams. Yum!

Escargot

Snails are served in fancy restaurants--it only proves that people will eat anything if it has enough butter and garlic on it. After a rain, take a bag, pillowcase, or brown bag and go out into the garden or city parks; gather the big ones. Usually, I stomp on them or throw them in the street to get run over by cars, because I am a gardener, and gardeners do not like snails. Exception! They are good to eat.

Get a plastic or glass container, sprinkle cornstarch in the bottom, cover with cheesecloth, and add the snails. And leave them for two days. This is called "purging;" it cleans their systems of anything they might have eaten in the garden that might poison you. Oh, and I suggest that you secure the cloth with a rubber band or string to prevent escapees.

After two days, rinse them off in cold water. If any appear to be dead, throw them away. After another two or three days, rinse them again in white vinegar and cold water. Now they are ready to cook.

Start a pot with enough water to cover them. Add a beer or some white wine. Bring to a boil and simmer for two hours until they're tender. Remove them and take the shells off by cracking them with a large knife and pulling the shells off as you would with an egg. In a pan, melt some butter, mince some garlic and add it, and put the snails in. Voila. You have escargot.

They're like shrimp. You have no qualms about eating shrimp, do you? Unless you are Sir Paul McCartney and don't eat anything with eyes.

Once upon a time, I decided to cultivate garden snails and make them bigger and fatter. I captured a few, kept them in a glass terrarium, fed them organic greens and cornmeal, and gave them fresh water every day. They thrived and laid eggs. (They look exactly like chicken eggs except they are teensy.) Eventually, the eggs hatched, and the cutest baby snails began following their parents around in a line, just the cutest thing you've ever seen. Well, I watched the family unite for a week and fell in love with them. I could not eat them after that. Sooo, I took them down the street and set them free in a neighbor's yard.

SWEETS

When I stayed with my grandmother, almost every summer, she would put me to bed before the sunset. After a while of not sleeping, I would come downstairs in my nightgown and say "I'm hungry." Mom would reach into the bread drawer and take out a loaf of bread she had baked that afternoon, slice off a large piece and cut it into small squares that she arranged in a shallow bowl. Then she would sprinkle it with white sugar and pour milk over it. It was the best dessert ever.

As promised earlier, here's the recipe I traded the chef for in Corpus Christi.

Jagger pie

1 graham-cracker crust pie shell

4 large avocados

1 can sweetened condensed milk

¼ cup lemon juice

Whipped cream to top

Put avocados, condensed milk, and lemon juice in a blender, and blend until smooth and creamy. Add more lemon to taste if you like it tart. Pour this into the piecrust, refrigerate at least an hour, and serve topped with whipped cream. It's unbelievably good--try it, you'll like it.

Pineapple upside-down cake
The first dessert I learned to make was an upside-down cake. As a child, I thought they were magic.

1 can sliced pineapple rings
1 stick butter
1 cup light brown sugar
Handful maraschino cherries
1 box cheap yellow cake mix

In a large cast iron pan, melt the butter, and then sprinkle brown sugar all over it. Place pineapple rings to cover the sugar, and put a maraschino cherry in each pineapple ring. (Maraschino cherries are full of red dye # 9 and are bad for you. So, feed it to the children. It won't kill them right away.) Mix up the cake according to the instructions on the box, and pour this mixture over the pineapple. Bake at 350 till the cake springs back when you touch it, or put a toothpick in it, and if it comes out clean, it is done.

Now gather the children around to watch this because this is where the magic happens. Get a plate larger than the pan, place it on top of the pan, and flip the two over together. Remove the pan carefully. Now you have a beautiful upside-down cake, and kids love it. I made one recently just for the fun of it. But with no kids around, it sat under the glass until it started to grow blue stuff. Then I fed it to the chickens.

Cookies

Once I made a pan of adult brownies and left them on the stove to cool, and Monah came home from school and ate them. She has not stopped talking about it; it adjusted her attitude for the day, maybe even her life.

Her favorite cookies are snickerdoodles, maybe because she just likes to say the word.

Thumbprints are my favorite because they are pretty

Raspberry thumbprints

You can use whatever jam you have on hand—strawberry, marmalade, and so forth.

¾ cup butter

¾ cup sugar

1 large egg

1 tsp. vanilla

2 cups flour

Cream the butter and sugar together, add the vanilla, sift in the flour, and mix well. Form into small round balls and arrange on a cookie sheet. Using your thumb, or a small thimble-size shot glass, make an indenture in the top of each cookie and put a teaspoon of jam into it. Be careful not to spill the jam on the pan; it sticks and is hard to clean. Bake till light gold--about 12 minutes. Wire baking racks are great for cooling cookies, but if you don't have one, just put them on paper towels or newspaper to cool; they look pretty on a nice plate.

Peanut butter cookies

I have timed myself, and I can make these cookies in 20 minutes--but then, I have made them a hundred million times.

1 cup granulated sugar

½ cup brown sugar

1 large egg

1 stick butter

1 tsp. vanilla

1 ½ cup flour

½ tsp. salt

½ tsp. baking powder

Preheat the oven to 350.

Cream the butter and sugar, add egg and vanilla until smooth, and then sift together the dry ingredients and add. Stir in a cup of peanut butter; I like crunchy, but you can use creamy.

Roll into little balls with your clean hands and place an inch apart on a greased baking pan. Then dip a fork into a little sugar and smash the fork into the little balls one way and then the other. This makes the small indentations that scream Peanut Butter Cookies. Bake for ten minutes. Don't overbake them. They will come out soft and crumbly but will firm up into scrumptious cookies, enough to fill a jar.

Martie's mom's soda cracker pie

Ever heard of anyone making homemade soda crackers? Didn't think so!

14 soda crackers

3 egg whites

1 cup sugar

1 1/2 tsp. vanilla

½ tsp. baking powder

½ cup chopped nuts

Crush the soda crackers. Beat the egg whites. Add sugar, vanilla, baking powder, nuts, and then the crackers. Grease a pie plate, pour everything in, and bake at 325 for 45 minutes. It's a bit strange but good. It was dry the first time I made it, so I added fresh berries. Then Martie said she forgot to tell me to cover it in whipped cream. Go figure! Now I think it's best with berries and whipped cream.

One April Fool's day. I mixed red food coloring with white vinegar and gelatin, poured it into little dessert cups, and stashed them in the fridge. Beau was the first to come from school. His eyes lit up when he opened the refrigerator. Oh boy, Jell-O. He grabbed a spoon and dug in. The look on his face was priceless. Before he went to the sink and spat it out, I shouted "April Fools!" "Ohhhh, that was dirty!" he said. Then his eyes lit up again. "Wait until Lisa gets here." So, he stood in the kitchen, waiting for the next victim. Lisa did the same thing. Then Nancy came in, and it was repeated. Though she cried... Not as much fun, but when she got over it, she joined in waiting for Monah. And we all got her. It was one of my best, and I hope they will repeat it with their children.

Traditions are valuable, like making cookies at Christmas. One year, sitting around the coffee table on cushions on the floor, in front of a crackling fire, all the kids were intent on decorating Christmas cookies with red, green, and white icing (powdered sugar and water). Beau was intent on a Santa boot; Monah, a Christmas tree; Lisa, an angel. And Nancy, what was she painting on that cookie? I knew what it looked like but had to ask—looking up from her handiwork with those big blue eyes, she smiled and said "spiders." Yes, that's what I thought.

FINAL THOUGHTS

After writing this, I went on to open not one but two restaurants, keeping the fun in it all. When seating a large party, I would give one person only the following menu and stand back and wait for the rest to order you can imagine. I loved the look on that person's face when one after the other ordered the number three and the number five.

In closing, remember--you are what you eat.

the NEW! Blue Frog
Food
Fun
Frivolity

STARTERS
May we suggest a tomato juice and Kahlua cocktail   32.75

SALADS
Poison Oak Salad with a Calamine dressing   16.23

Entrees

Squid lovely sautéed in bubble bubble gum sauce   22

Poached salmon Just don't tell the game warden   22

Real rat tat tutie taste like chicken

Road kill special What ever we hit coming down the hill   25

ASK ABOUT OUR PENGUIN TACOS   **Market price**

CALAVERAS COUNTY FROGS LEGS Available only after   5.94
frog jump

WORM BURGER Just like Wendy's use to make   13.69

STEVENOT STEAK Tough as hell but goes down nicely with   59.95
two bottles of cab.

PEANUT BUTTER AND JELLY SANDWICH   200.00

SPINACH AND GRASSHOPPER RAVIOLI   1.00

ABSOULTELEY STONED CATFISH
Steamed in bathtub gin and vermouth   18.00

Printed in the United States
By Bookmasters